Restaurant Promotion through Social Media

Table of Contents

We don't have a choice on whether we do social
media, the question is how well we do it.

Chapter 1. Introduction

Unveil the secrets of savvy social media marketing in the restaurant industry with our compelling Special Report: "Restaurant Promotion through Social Media!" This isn't your typical, dull, statistics-overloaded report. Oh no, this lively, engaging page-turner is packed full of real-world case studies, practical strategies, and expert insights designed to supercharge your restaurant's social media presence. Whether you manage a cozy corner bistro or a sprawling food franchise, this report offers invaluable tips and tricks to win over the online crowd. So, get ready to serve up mouth-watering content, dish out irresistible offers, and transform your social media diners into devoted, raving fans. Grab your copy of this essential guide today and start your journey towards becoming the talk of the digital town!

Chapter 2. The Power of Social Media in the Restaurant Industry

The new age of digital communication isn't just changing the way individuals socialize. It has dramatically altered the dynamics of numerous industries, including the restaurant industry. With the swift growth of social media platforms, restaurants now have an unprecedented opportunity to communicate and engage with a vast audience. The landscape of restaurant marketing isn't simply about billboards, radio spots, or TV commercials anymore. It's about Twitter engagements, Instagram stories, Facebook likes, YouTube videos, and more. The power of social media in driving restaurant businesses towards success cannot be underestimated.

2.1. Social Media: A Powerful Tool for Restaurant Promotions

In the digital era, social media has emerged as a major player for restaurant promotional activities. It's a pivotal instrument for shaping customer perceptions, fortifying brand loyalty, and attracting new customers. When used strategically, a simple tweet or an Instagram story can become a powerful marketing tool, setting a domino effect in motion that may lead to bookings, orders, and brand recognition.

Restaurant owners nowadays are leveraging the power of networking and sharing on social media platforms to showcase their food offerings, build a close-knit community, and stand out from the competition. The ease of shareability and interactivity on these platforms amplifies the reach of promotional content, creating a ripple effect.

2.2. Role of Social Media in Customer Engagement

Customer engagement lies at the heart of any restaurant business. Social media platforms offer something that traditional mediums do not—interactivity. Whether it's a string of heart emojis left in the comment section or a photo of a perfectly plated dish shared by a customer, social media provides a platform for direct communication and engagement with the audience.

This two-way communication helps restaurants not only to communicate their brand message more effectively but also to gain crucial insights from customers' responses and preferences. Customers feel heard and valued, building a sense of community around the brand.

2.3. Boosting Brand Awareness through Social Media

Social media is one of the most effective tools to increase brand awareness due to its broad reach. By consistently presenting engaging and informative content, a restaurant can mold its online persona and introduce itself to online users who might not be aware of the business.

Strategies like hashtagging, collaboration with influencers, and participating in trending topics or challenges can significantly increase visibility. Social platforms also enable users to share the restaurant's content, leading to widespread exposure even beyond the restaurant's immediate follower base.

2.4. Harnessing User-Generated Content (UGC)

User-Generated Content is like a gold mine for restaurants. A food lover clicking a picture of their meal and posting it on social media is one of the most authentic ways of marketing. Not only does it amplify the reach of the restaurant's brand, but it also introduces a level of authenticity and trustworthiness that can't be achieved through traditional marketing techniques. UGC holds immense power in drawing more customers to the restaurant, by creating a FOMO (Fear of Missing Out) effect.

2.5. Social Media as an Analytical Tool

The beauty of social media lies in the fact that it is not just a broadcasting tool, but also an analytical one. Restaurants can measure engagement rates, audience growth, conversion rates, etc., to gauge the performance of their social media strategy. This data provides valuable insights into customer preferences and behavior, enabling restaurants to further customize their offerings and marketing strategies for maximum results.

The emergence of social media has radically transformed the marketing strategies in the restaurant industry, compelling businesses to adapt and evolve. By harnessing the power of social media, restaurants are managing to increase their visibility, foster customer relationships, and ultimately, boost their bottom lines. The ongoing digital revolution continues to set new norms and trends, and the restaurants that keep pace by integrating social in their marketing mix stand to gain the most.

In the following chapters, we will delve deeper into understanding the different social media platforms and their unique offerings, effective strategies for creating compelling content, leveraging user-generated content, mastering social advertising, and much more. Buckle up as we set off on this exciting journey to explore the world of social media marketing in the restaurant industry.

Chapter 3. Understanding Social Media Platforms: From Twitter to TikTok

The thrilling world of social media is vast and varied, offering a multitude of different platforms each peopled with their own devoted audience. As a restaurant owner or marketer, you must be capable of deciphering these platforms, recognizing their particularities, and ultimately, advantageously employing them towards your promotional intentions.

3.1. Twitter: Engage and Inform in 280 Characters

Tweeting may seem a soundbite micro-discipline, yet Twitter's reliance on brevity does not undermine its capacity for deep engagement. Twitter allows for real-time conversation with your patrons, catering for promotion, complaints, praise, or general chitchat, uniquely humanizing your brand. Sharing morsels of interesting news or behind-the-scenes tidbits can encourage brand enthusiasm, while retweeting and acknowledging favorable customer reviews promotes a palpable sense of camaraderie.

Tips on how to use Twitter for your restaurant: - Regularly tweet appealing food photos. - Retweet positive customer feedback. - Share behind-the-scenes glimpses into your restaurant. - Run time-bound Twitter-exclusive offers, creating an exciting sense of urgency.

3.2. Facebook: Cultivating Community with a Personal Touch

Equipped with a wealth of features, Facebook remains a crucial component of any restaurant's social media strategy. Facebook Page is your restaurant's own digital home, showcasing your menu, location, operating hours, and photos, while facilitating direct communication with your patrons. The usefulness of Facebook groups in fostering an intimate sense of community around your brand cannot be overstated.

Tips for leveraging Facebook: - Post photos and videos of dishes, events, and happy diners. - Share blog posts or articles about your restaurant. - Use Facebook live features to host interactive Q&A sessions. - Create a dedicated Facebook group for your regular patrons.

3.3. Instagram: Telling Stories Through Pictures

Instagram reigns supreme in the realm of visual storytelling. Its image-heavy interface is ideal for flaunting appetizing dishes, stunning decor or your friendly staff. Quality photos shot in good light can pique interest and stimulate cravings, while Instagram stories offer a causal platform for sharing ephemeral content of your restaurant's daily hustle and bustle.

Tips for using Instagram effectively: - Share high-quality pictures and videos of your food. - Use Instagram Stories to showcase your team or daily operations. - Follow, share, and comment on customers' posts featuring your restaurant. - Use relevant hashtags to increase post visibility.

3.4. TikTok: Creativity Unleashed

Embracing the TikTok revolution provides an unrivalled opportunity to display your restaurant's creative side and target a younger demographic. Short-form video content elicits amusement, amazement, and engagement, making it ideal for generating viral moments. Behind-the-scenes kitchen clips, step-by-step recipe videos, or fun staff snippets could amass a swarm of interested followers.

Tips to make TikTok work for your restaurant: - Share humorous and entertaining short videos. - Participate in viral challenges or trending memes relevant to your industry. - Record time-lapse videos of food preparation. - Collaborate with popular TikTok influencers.

The secret to successful social media marketing lies in the fine balance between platform diversity and specificity. Each platform offers unique ways to engage customers, and understanding how to creatively leverage these features while maintaining a consistent brand voice across all platforms is your keystone to success. Engage, communicate, and exhibit authenticity, and the realm of social media will become a thriving digital home for your restaurant.

Chapter 4. Building Your Brand Identity on Social Media

Crafting a robust and compelling social media presence for your restaurant involves far more than simply setting up accounts on various platforms and posting occasional updates. It requires the development of an all-encompassing brand identity that resonates with your audience and distinguishes your establishment from the competition. This not only influences how your customers perceive your restaurant, but it also contributes to their emotional connection with your offerings.

4.1. Crafting a Unique Brand Voice

Your brand voice is an integral aspect of your brand identity. It personifies your brand, making it relatable to your target audience. When creating your brand voice, consider the unique qualities that make your restaurant stand out. This could include everything from the type of food you serve, to your restaurant's history, or the way you present your dishes. Be sure to incorporate these aspects into your content, ensuring that your voice resonates throughout everything you do. Remember, consistency is key. Using the same tone and style in all your posts will help strengthen your brand identity and build trust with your audience.

4.2. Articulating Your Brand Values

Just as important as your brand voice are your brand values, or the principles that your restaurant stands for. When sharing any content on social media, make sure it aligns with your values. Engage with customers, staff, and even the wider community in a manner that reflects these values. This might mean showcasing locally sourced ingredients to highlight your commitment to sustainability, or regularly posting about charity events to show your dedication to community engagement.

4.3. Creating Consistent Visual Identity

Visual identity plays a crucial role in defining your social media presence. It goes beyond your restaurant's logo, branching out into color palettes, typefaces used in your posts, presentation of your dishes, and even the style and tone of images you share on social media. All these aspects work collectively to create a cohesive, recognizable image of your brand. You could experiment by sharing behind-the-scenes photos, showcasing your culinary team in action, or highlighting the ingredients you use in your dishes. Remember, all the imagery you use–whether it's in poster promotions or in your posts–needs to align with your overall brand aesthetics.

4.4. Connecting with Customers through Stories

The way you interact with your customers on social media can significantly impact your brand identity. Always strive to connect with your audience on a personal level. One great way to do this is by sharing stories–both your own and your customers'. You might share the journey of your restaurant, interesting facts about your menu items, or simply highlight customer testimonials. Remember, your customers want to feel like they're a part of your journey, and authentic storytelling can bridge the gap between you and your customers.

4.5. Leveraging User-Generated Content

Lastly, user-generated content (UGC) can be a game-changer for your restaurant's social media branding. Encourage your customers to share their experiences at your restaurant on social media. They can post pictures of your dishes, share positive experiences, or even spread the word about how much they love your brand. This not only magnifies the reach of your brand but also adds credibility to your restaurant's reputation as people tend to trust reviews and content created by other consumers.

In essence, building brand identity through social media is all about fostering a relationship with your audience–a relationship built on trust, consistency, and engagement. It's about representing your restaurant in a way that's true to what you stand for, and making your audience feel like they're a part of your community. By integrating your restaurant's unique qualities into your social media content, telling engaging stories, maintaining a strong visual identity, and leveraging user-generated content, you stand to create a thriving social media presence that can take your restaurant to new heights.

Chapter 5. Cooking up Content: Creating Posts that Engage and Inspire

Creating engaging content on social media is akin to perfecting a recipe. It calls for a balanced blend of catchy visuals, powerful narratives, and valuable insights, all garnished with a pinch of fun and personality. This chapter is a step-by-step guide for cooking up irresistible content that will not only catch attention, but also inspire your audience to engage, share and return for more.

5.1. Deconstructing the Ingredient List: Understanding Your Audience

Before you can begin crafting any form of content, it's essential to understand who will be at the receiving end of your message - your audience. Investing time in audience analysis allows you to uncover what your customers value in a dining experience, their cuisine preferences, dietary restrictions, and the type of content they find most engaging. This data becomes your content 'ingredient list', helping you build content strategies aligned with your customers' tastes.

5.2. Recipe for Success: Defining Your Content Strategy

Once you've defined who you're talking to, it's time to determine what you need to say and how best to say it. This phase requires developing a solid content strategy, a structured plan to guide your content creation efforts. Your strategy should include considerations for the right social media platforms, frequency and timing of posts, tailoring your messages to specific demographics, and planning for special campaigns or events.

5.3. Mastering the Food Presentation: Visual Content is Key

In an industry that thrives on sensory experiences, the visual appeal of your posts is paramount. High-quality images and videos of mouth-watering dishes can make your audience's taste buds tingle from miles away. Showcase the culinary skills and creativity of your kitchen team, the ambiance of your dining space, or the experiences of your diners. Consider a visual content style guide to maintain a consistent and recognizable presence that's unique to your brand.

5.4. Seasoning Your Content: Adding Personality & Value

A vital aspect of engaging content is that it must offer value to the viewer, and a personalized touch can make this value tangible. This means going beyond simply selling your product or service, and instead providing insightful, educational, or entertaining content. It could be a behind-the-scenes look at your restaurant, a cooking tutorial from your chef, or a moment of a happy customer. Build a brand personality that resonates with your audience, showcasing authenticity and promoting a genuine connection.

5.5. Mixing it Right: Variety in Your Content Mix

Variety is the spice of social media content. Mixing up your content will not only keep your audience engaged but also cater to varying interests. Consider creating a content mix that includes recipes, promotional announcements, customer testimonials, staff bios or fun kitchen mess-ups. Adding novelty to your content mix with limited-time or seasonal offerings, special events, or partnerships with local businesses can also be a winning idea.

5.6. The Garnish: Call-to-Actions & Engaging Prompts

Like the perfect garnish to a scrumptious dish, a well-crafted call-to-action (CTA) can add the final touch to your content. A compelling CTA guides your audience on the next steps, whether it's making a reservation, participating in a contest, or sharing your content. Encourage user-generated content by asking your followers to share photos of their meal or experiences at your restaurant. This can augment your content while fostering a sense of community.

5.7. Analyzing & Adjusting Your Recipe: The Importance of Analytics

As you serve up enticing content, it's essential to analyze your performance regularly. Use social media analytics to measure the effectiveness of your posts. Watch out for trends in likes, shares, comments, and follower growth, as well as peak engagement times and demographics. Based on this data, fine-tune your content recipe to further resonate with your audience, optimize performance, and maximum ROI.

Remember that the realm of social media marketing is dynamic and evolving. What worked yesterday may not work tomorrow. Keep experimenting, innovating, and integrating customer feedback into your social media content strategy to stay fresh and relevant. Creating engaging, inspiring content is an art that requires patience, creativity, and a keen understanding of your audience. Approach it like you would a new recipe, with an open mind and a willingness to try different methods to achieve that perfect balance of ingredients.

Chapter 6. Making the Most of User-Generated Content

Content that sprouts organically from the people who love your brand, patrons who engage and interact with your restaurant online, weave the energy and fibre of user-generated content (UGC). Harnessed carefully and smartly, this content can be a powerful tool in your digital marketing arsenal to stimulate exponential growth in your social media popularity and influence.

6.1. Understanding User-Generated Content

User-generated content is any form of content, such as images, videos, text, and audio, that has been posted by users on online platforms such as social media and wikis. In the context of a restaurant, user-generated content can come in infinitely diverse forms: A perfectly filtered Instagram post of your signature paella, a glowing Facebook review about your attentive waitstaff, an enthusiastic tweet raving about your unique ambiance, or even an aesthetically pleasing TikTok video featuring your artisanal cocktails. These are all forms of UGC; they establish and shape your online presence, shaping perceptions of your brand from the grassroots.

6.2. Why Leveraging User-Generated Content is Vital

It's clear that UGC has an essential role in the socio-digital landscape, but just why is it so important to incorporate into your promotional campaign? Here's why:

Relatability: Your customers trust their peers more than they trust your brand. Peer opinions often sway potential diners more than any form of direct advertising.

Authenticity: UGC aids in building a genuine brand. It's authentic, real, and raw, revealing a candid representation of what your establishment brings to the table.

Cost-effective: UGC is a great way to share content without substantial resource allocation. By repurposing this content, you can maintain a constant stream of posts without spending a fortune.

More comprehensive: UGC shows different aspects of your business that you might not have thought to highlight. Customers capture moments that they resonate with, which might be different from what you emphasize.

6.3. How to Encourage User-Generated Content

There are a few effective methods to stimulate a constant flow of UGC.

Competitions: Announce a photo contest where the participant posts a picture of your dish with your defined hashtag. It could be a free meal or merchandise.

Incentives: Offer incentives such as discounts or freebies to customers who share a post about your restaurant.

Featured posts: Select some user posts every week and share them on your social networks giving credit to the original poster. It encourages other users to share their experiences in hopes of being featured.

User centric events: Arrange events that encourage patrons to share content online such as interactive cooking classes, tastings or meet the chef nights.

6.4. Making the Most of the Posted Content

Once you've encouraged the creation of user-generated content for your restaurant, ensure its mileage goes beyond just the user's followers.

Feature on Your Channels: Sharing customer posts on your official social media channels gives it a larger audience, and also shows acknowledgement and appreciation to the original poster.

Create a UGC Gallery: Dedicate a space on your website or social media platform for a UGC gallery. It not only showcases customer experiences, but also serves as a compelling testament of your brand's popularity.

Promote with Hashtags: Create a branded hashtag for your UGC campaign. It can segue into a trending topic on social media and encourages further patron participation.

Crisis Management: Be prepared to manage negative UGC, which, despite its potential to sway public opinion negatively, can also be an opportunity to show your exceptional customer service.

In summary, user-generated content is a profound and influential aspect of your restaurant's social media promotion. It not only boosts the trust factor, but also shapes brand perception through its authenticity, relatability, and cost-effectiveness. It's a potent tool in your digital marketing kit, and understanding how to tap into the potential of UGC can redefine your online presence and solidify your foothold in the market. Defining a vibrant and engaging UGC campaign can open up new avenues in customer interaction, brand promotion, and business growth. So, tuck in your digital marketing bib, dust off your hashtags, and prep your social media platforms - it's time to dine on the feast of user-generated content!

Chapter 7. Social Media Promotions: Nailing the Right Strategy

From the very emergence of social media platforms, businesses have had to adapt in order to continue reaching their consumers effectively. By now, it's indisputable that a well-executed social media strategy has the potential to spiral a restaurant's popularity, increase customer engagement and effectively promote the brand. The key, however, lies in the execution. Nailing the right strategy can be daunting, but with insight, planning, and the right approach, you could easily be on your way to a successful social media campaign that aligns with your overall business goals.

7.1. Understanding Your Target Audience

Before we delve into the numerous strategies available for promotion via social media, it is absolutely crucial to establish a clear understanding of your target audience. You must learn to speak their language and appeal to their interests if you're to capture their attention and keep them coming to your restaurant. Start by asking yourself a few basic questions about the likely demographic makeup of your customers. Questions could range from the simple 'What age group do they fall under?' to the more complex 'What type of content do they usually engage with on social media?' The answers you unravel would provide a solid foundation upon which you can build a tailor-made promotional strategy.

7.2. What Makes You Stand Out?

Now that you've familiarized yourself with who your audience is, the next step is to identify what sets your business apart. What about your restaurant makes it unique? Is it the cozy ambiance, the secret sauce, the multicuisine menu, the live events, or the spectacular view? Your marketing strategies should aim at painting an attractive picture of these unique features, evoking curiosity and interest in your audience.

7.3. Choosing the Right Platforms

It's all good and well to know your audience and what makes your restaurant special, but none of it matters unless you have an understanding of where to reach your audience. Some businesses make the mistake of trying to establish a presence on every conceivable social media platform. It's best to remember that what works incredibly for one restaurant may not necessarily work for another. Consider the general user demographic of each platform. Instagram and Snapchat, for instance, bear a younger user base, while Facebook and LinkedIn draw an older one. Perhaps Twitter is where your tech-savvy audience hangs out, or Tiktok is where your trendy crowd turns to. It's not about being everywhere; it's about being where your customers are.

7.4. Crafting Engaging Content

Remember, content is king! The type of content shared will call the shots in effective social media promotion. It's time to whip up a recipe for engaging content to entice your audience! Including a few tasty visuals of your dishes, captivating captions, sharing customer testimonials and sharing your behind-the-scenes stories could add the kind of flavor that keeps your audience yearning for more. Providing valuable, relatable, and engaging content fosters a connection with your audience, making them feel like part of your restaurant's story.

7.5. Incorporating User-Generated Content

A stellar strategy to maximize your reach and engagement is to incorporate user-generated content. Encourage your customers to share their experiences at your restaurant, maybe even run an interactive competition where customers can share creative pictures or videos taken at your restaurant for a chance to win a prize. Not only does this provide you with a constant stream of fresh content, but it is also an excellent way to build trust and loyalty among your existing customers and attract potential ones.

7.6. Effective Use of Hashtags

Hashtags serve the dual purpose of making your content discoverable by nudging it under the umbrella of similar content and allowing you to track discussions centered around your brand. Creating a unique and catchy hashtag for your restaurant can encourage customers to use it when they share their experiences, effectively amplifying the reach of your brand.

7.7. Time Your Posts

Each social media platform has unique peak times when users' activities are at their highest. Timing your posts to coincide with these peak times ensures that your posts reach as many users as possible, therefore rendering you maximum engagement.

7.8. Analyze, Adjust and Keep up

Finally, remember to assess the performance of your strategies regularly. The social media world is constantly evolving. Stay updated with the latest trends and ensure that your strategies align accordingly. You might need to modify a few things here and there — a slight adjustment in content type, a shift in post timings, an updated promotional strategy. What matters is to keep up with the changes and bring your 'A' game to the floor!

Exploring the vast landscape of social media might seem overwhelming at first, but with a deep understanding of your target audience and the right strategies, it can prove to be a game-changer in your restaurant's promotional endeavors. Remember to keep the content engaging, the promotions exciting and the engagement, constant. Go ahead! Your online crowds are waiting to be amazed!

Chapter 8. Using Online Reviews and Ratings to Your Advantage

Online reviews and ratings can act as a powerful modulator for the trajectory of your restaurant's reputation and popularity amongst a spectrum of diverse patrons online. Harnessing and leveraging these digital opinion vectors, with their far-reaching consequences, can inevitably help your establishment succeed in the competitive realm of the restaurant industry.

8.1. Online Reviews and Ratings: The Double-Edged Sword

A fundamental understanding of the nature of online reviews and ratings and how they directly affect your restaurant's visibility is necessary in order to effectively leverage them. While positive reviews can propel your establishment into the limelight, expose your restaurant to a larger audience, and increase the likelihood of visits from new customers; negative reviews can decrease your establishment's visibility, tarnish its reputation, and potentially drive away prospective diners. Hence, it is crucial to monitor these reviews and frequently respond to them, ensuring a consistent communication channel between your restaurant and its patrons.

8.2. Strategies to Solicit Positive Reviews

1. Request for Reviews: Train your staff to casually encourage satisfied customers to leave reviews after their dining experience. Including a small note suggesting the same along

with the bill can serve as a gentle nudge.

2. Run Contests and Offers: Host contests on your social media platforms, offering discounts or complimentary meals for a selected number of customers who leave detailed reviews.

3. Leverage Technology: Use restaurant management software that seamlessly asks your customers for reviews via SMS or email after their visit.

8.3. Dealing with Negative Reviews and Ratings

No restaurant can escape negative reviews completely. The crucial aspect is how you address them. A few strategies to manage negative feedback effectively are:

1. Always Respond: Always reply to negative comments, showing that you value the customer's opinion, and are ready to improve.

2. Apologize and Rectify: If the problem stated in the review was indeed a fault on your part, accept it. Apologize, offer a solution, or invite the customer to try your service again.

3. Private Communication: Whenever possible, take the conversation offline or to a private chat where you can interact with the customer directly.

4. Leverage them as Constructive Criticism: Use negative reviews to understand the areas of your service that need improvement.

8.4. Utilizing Good Reviews and Ratings

The impact of good reviews extends beyond their immediate effect. Utilize them in your marketing strategy to attract more customers.

You can:

1. Showcase Reviews: Highlight positive reviews on your social media platforms. Do not forget to thank the customers in your posts.

2. Display Reviews-Influenced Content: Create engaging content like infographics and short video clips around the positive feedback.

3. Leverage them for Improved Ranking: High ratings improve your position on review sites, making your restaurant more visible.

With tactful handling, online reviews and ratings can be a boon to your restaurant's digital presence. They generate valuable user-generated content while acting as a mirror reflecting the strengths and weaknesses of your restaurant. The strategies provided in this chapter offer a robust and sophisticated roadmap for leveraging online reviews and ratings to your restaurant's advantage. By following these instructions meticulously, you can gear your dining establishment towards a path of digital glory, inviting rave reviews, and elevating ratings.

Chapter 9. Mastering Social Media Advertising for Restaurant Promotions

In the ever-connected world we live in, social media advertising holds an immense power to shape perceptions, guide consumer behavior, and ultimately, drive business growth for your restaurant. To tap into this vast potential, you need more than just a basic understanding of popular platforms and their algorithms. You need a concrete, comprehensive plan tailored to your specific offerings, capturing the unique essence that sets your eatery apart from the crowd.

9.1. The Fundamental Aspects of Social Media Advertising

Diving into the depths of social media advertising, it's crucial to comprehend the various components that form its foundation. These include:

- Selecting the right platform(s) for your advertising campaign

- Understanding the algorithm and how content promotion works on these platforms

- Identifying your target audience and crafting content that resonates with them

- Determining your advertising budget and optimizing for cost effectiveness

- Tracking campaign performance and applying data-driven improvements

Each of these facets is an essential cog in the machine that helps power your restaurant's online promotional efforts. A thorough understanding and adept navigation of these components can significantly increase your chances of crafting highly successful social media advertising campaigns.

9.2. Choosing the Right Social Media Platform for Your Ad Campaigns

Just as different kinds of food appeal to different people, your choice of platform should be dictated by where your target audience is most active. Statistics and audience demographics offer valuable insights here. For instance, Instagram, with its focus on visually appealing posts, serves as a fitting platform for showcasing mouthwatering images of your culinary creations, behind-the-scenes peeks and promotions. On the other hand, Facebook, due to its universal appeal and extensive user demographics, provides a broad canvas for ads, events, and promotions.

Moreover, platforms like TikTok, with a largely younger audience and its predilection for eye-catching, bite-sized videos, can be used to share quick cooking tips, restaurant tours or quirky bits of your staff showing off their culinary skills - all of which act as mini promotional segments for your business.

9.3. Understanding Social Media Advertising Algorithms

Advertising on social media isn't just about crafting compelling content; it's also about understanding platform algorithms to maximize reach and engagement. While algorithms consistently evolve, most tend to prioritize content that encourages interaction, shares, comments, and time spent on the post. Therefore, devising ads that intrigue, entertain, educate, or inspire can potentially generate more engagement and hence, better visibility in the ever-competitive social media landscape.

9.4. Crafting a Compelling Advertising Narrative

At the heart of your advertising campaign lies the narrative or the story you choose to relay. Whether it's the inspiration behind your signature dish, the procurement of locally sourced ingredients, or the warmth of your cordial staff, choose a narrative that's unique to your restaurant. Your ad copy should reflect this narrative in a compelling manner, sparkling curiosity and interest among viewers.

9.5. Budgeting Your Ad Campaigns and Ensuring Cost-Effectiveness

It's also crucial to allocate a specific budget for your advertising efforts and monitor the Cost Per Click (CPC) or Cost Per Impression (CPM), depending on your campaign goals. Early testing in limited segments can help gauge potential response rates and tweak your campaign for better performance. Remember, your goal should not just be to reach a wider audience but to ensure this reach is effective, enhancing brand awareness and driving conversions.

9.6. Leveraging the Power of Social Media Analytics

Understanding how to decipher and apply data from social media analytics to your future campaigns is another crucial aspect of mastering social media ad promotions. These analytics can offer insights into what worked and what didn't, providing you guidance to replicate success and avoid pitfalls in future campaigns.

Mastering social media advertising for restaurant promotions is an ongoing venture, with twists and turns at every corner. However, a well-planned and analytically driven advertising strategy can be an indispensable tool in your promotional arsenal. Packed with intelligence and innovation, it holds a potential not just to appease the digital appetites of your audience, but to consistently satiate them, transforming casual viewers into fervent advocates for your culinary haven.

Chapter 10. Associating with Influencers: Leveraging their Reach

The restaurant industry has grown enormously over the years, but it has also ventured into different methods of marketing and advertising. Social media has been a strong channel for restaurants, and influencers are playing a significant role in this outing.

10.1. Understanding Influencer Marketing in the Restaurant Industry

Influencer marketing is the modern-day word-of-mouth advertising, where influencers, renowned individuals with a substantial social media following, recommend your restaurant to their followers.

Several studies indicate a significant return on investment (ROI) from influencer marketing. According to a study by Tomoson, businesses make around $6.50 for every dollar spent on influencer marketing. This proves that using influencers for restaurant promotion can yield significant results.

10.2. How to Identify the Right Influencers

Not all influencers will be right for your restaurant. Savvy restaurant marketers need to consider several factors including the influencer's niche and the alignment with their brand, their reach, their engagement rate, and their audience demographics.

A food blogger might not be the best fit for a fine dining restaurant, and a celebrity with millions of followers might not be the right advocate for a cozy, family-run cafe. Understanding these dynamics is necessary to unlock the potential of influencer marketing.

10.3. Building Relationships with Influencers

Once the right influencers have been identified, the next step is to build a relationship with them. This could involve inviting them for a meal at your restaurant, sending them some signature dishes, or even arranging a behind-the-scenes tour. The idea is to provide them with a unique experience that they will want to share with their followers.

10.4. Creating Collaborative Content

The content created with influencers is crucial, as it would shape the audience's perception of your establishment. This could involve a cooking session with your head chef, a Q&A session, a food tasting vlog, or simply a candid picture of the influencer dining at your restaurant. The content should reflect the identity of your brand and resonate with the followers of the influencer.

10.5. Measuring the Impact of Influencer Marketing

Measuring the impact of influencer marketing can be tricky but is an essential part of the process. You can track metrics such as the reach of the post, engagement rate, increased follower count, and, in some cases, the increase in reservations or walk-ins resulting from the influencer's promotion. This data will provide valuable insights into the effectiveness of your influencer marketing strategies.

10.6. Overcoming Challenges and Turning Them Into Opportunities

Despite the abundant benefits, influencer marketing in the restaurant industry isn't devoid of challenges. Authenticity could be at risk if influencer partnerships are perceived as purely transactional. However, by aligning with influencers who genuinely love and patronize your restaurant, you can ensure an authentic connection that followers will trust and appreciate. The key is to find an influencer who likes your brand and sees value in building a long-term relationship.

In conclusion, influencer marketing is an efficacious tool in the restaurant industry that can unlock massive visibility and following. It requires a blend of strategic thinking, relationship building, creative content creation, and continuous performance tracking to ensure optimal results. By associating with influencers and leveraging their reach, restaurant marketers can connect with a wider audience and enhance the overall reputation of their brand. Building the right partnership and investing in the right strategies would ensure your plate on the digital space is always full and delicious.

Chapter 11. Crisis Management on Social Media: Handling Negative Feedback

In the modern age of high-speed communication and unprecedented accessibility to feedback channels, crisis management on social media and handling negative feedback has become a critical aspect of a restaurant's operation. It is not so much a question of if a crisis will occur, but rather when it will, and how your restaurant should handle it.

11.1. Understanding the Power of Negative Feedback

Negative feedback, while often viewed as a threat, holds hidden power. It acts as a mirror reflecting its flaws that a restaurant may have overlooked. When a customer expresses their dissatisfaction online, they do so with the perception of their experience. Whether it's about the food, service, or ambiance, it pinpoints precisely where your restaurant didn't meet their expectations.

In the age where a single online review can greatly influence a potential customer's purchasing decision, paying attention and addressing negative feedback is not merely optional—it's absolutely essential. But how do you turn negatives into positives? How do you manage these crises effectively?

11.2. The Art of Dealing with Negative Reviews

When faced with a negative review, it's easy to take the defensive. But remember, everyone's watching how you respond. The rule of thumb is acknowledging the reviewer's feelings, showing empathy, and addressing the issue promptly and professionally. It is this kind of respectful engagement that can actually turn a dissatisfied customer into a loyal one.

Instead of trying to justify the circumstances, demonstrate your commitment to improvement. This may mean admitting errors, explaining what went wrong, and most importantly, outlining what actions will be taken to avoid such instances in the future. Every complaint is an opportunity to learn and improve. But remember to always keep your responses public, so other potential customers see that you're actively addressing concerns and taking feedback seriously.

11.3. Ensuring Effective Crisis Management

The key to successfully navigating a crisis lies in proactively preparing for one. Develop a crisis communication plan that outlines the necessary steps to be taken when managing negative feedback. This plan should also define the roles within your team.

Transparency, speed of response, and effective communication are essential elements of an effective crisis management strategy. Keep a planned response template ready for recurring issues, but remember to always personalize the response to show genuine concern. The timelier your response, the higher the chances of diffusing the situation before it escalates.

Monitor your restaurant's social media presence continually to spot issues early. Social media listening tools can help watch the conversation about your restaurant on various platforms. This way, you can identify potential crises before they blow up, and deal with negative feedback promptly.

11.4. Learning from Negative Feedback: Continual Improvement

Above all, negative feedback offers a unique opportunity for growth and learning. It highlights areas that may be failing or underperforming. Remember, feedback comes from the core: your customers. They are the ones who experience your dishes, service, and atmosphere firsthand.

Analyzing feedback can deliver new insights, pointing to practical steps for improvement. Discuss feedback in regular team meetings, emphasizing the significance of service quality and customer satisfaction.

To conclude, dealing with crises and negative feedback is much more than putting out fires in the digital world. It entails a profound understanding of customer perceptions, expectations, and experiences. It is about learning, adapting, and striving for continual improvement on the go, ensuring the restaurant keeps up with the fast-paced and ever-evolving dynamics of the restaurant industry in the digital age.